I Love Big Machines

BY: MELISSA WHITTINGTON

THIS BOOK IS FOR BRAYDEN,
WHO COULD PRONOUNCE
EXCAVATOR WHEN HE WAS TWO.

Tractor: This tractor works on the farm, helping with plowing and moving heavy things.

Excavator:
It digs deep
holes and
moves lots
of dirt.

Dump Truck: This truck carries heavy loads, like dirt and rocks, and tips them out.

Bulldozer:
A strong machine with a blade in front that pushes things out of the way.

**Cement Mixer:
This truck spins
round and round,
making concrete
for building things.**

Crane:
A tall machine
with a long arm
to lift and move
heavy stuff.

Backhoe Loader:
This machine digs
with a big bucket
in the back and
scoops with a
smaller one in the
front.

Road Roller:
It's heavy and
rolls over the road
to make it smooth
and flat.

Forklift:
This machine
lifts and moves
heavy things
with its front
arms.

Skid Steer Loader:
A small machine that turns quickly and is good for tight spaces.

Concrete Pump Truck:

It's like a tall truck with a long arm that pours concrete in high places.

Front Loader:
A big truck with a scoop in front that picks up and carries things.

Compactor:
This machine
presses down on
the ground to
make it hard and
flat.

Paver:
A truck that spreads and smoothens hot asphalt to make roads.

Scraper:
A machine that scrapes and moves dirt from one place to another.

Trencher:
It digs long,
narrow holes in
the ground,
like a big
shovel.

Good
Bye